Sheba's Jam:

Lessons from Roller Derby and Life

Written By
Janine Folks

Sheba's Jam

Sheba's Jam: Lessons From Roller Derby and Life
By Janine Folks

ISBN- 978-0-97015-916-8
© 2015, 2021 by Janine Folks

Unless otherwise noted, all scripture is from the *King James Version* of the Bible.

Cover design: D. H. Art Design: www.dhartdesign.net

Cover photo credit: Phil Connor Images (PCI)

Book coordination by: www.getthepen.net

SHEBA'S JAM

Dedication

*In loving memory of beloveds: my sister Lynette Folks
and dear friend Sandra Dobson*

*In celebration, honor and acknowledgement of all
female athletes, past, present and future.*

My Maker

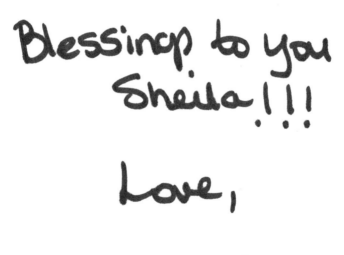

Blessings to you
Sheila!!!

Love,

Janine

SHEBA'S JAM
The Inspiration

A great portion of this book was inspired by lessons I learned and things I observed during my two season stint with a women's roller derby league. Playing Roller Derby in my 40's (2013 - 2015). It was a great adventure and confidence booster. It was life changing.

I took some things I learned in Roller Derby and drew parallels to my many years of studying the Bible. Some principles are universal. This book is an attempt to articulate my observations and conclusions, merging the mind of a Bible student Preacher/Writer and a derby girl.

A few parts of this book were inspired by roller skating, roller derby and other sport related activities as well as everyday life. My mind is always drawing parallels and this book gives you a glimpse into how I think and process my experiences.

I hope these words bless you.

Sheba's Jam
Table of contents

Sheba's Jam

Sheba's Jam

Preface
If you are familiar with my writing, it needs no introduction. If this is the first time you are reading my work, you will be introduced as you read. In short, this is why I write.

Purpose
To change the world through the ministry of writing by discussing relevant issues and challenges and presenting solutions through Bible scripture. This is done by way of writing, publishing, marketing and distributing inspirational books.

Philosophy
The Holy Bible, God's Word, is the foundation of our edification, enlightenment, exhortation and encouragement. It is also a blessing to be able to read books that help us to apply Bible principles to our situations and feelings. Good Christian books are like written preaching. When we read, our spirit hears. The Bible asks, "How shall they hear without a preacher? And how shall they preach unless they are sent?" (Romans 10:14-15).

Mission
To promote the Gospel of Jesus Christ through inspirational writing by inspiration of God through His Word and by His Spirit!

SHEBA'S JAM
A Tribute to Lynette Folks

My sister in law, whom I affectionately called, "My Sister" died unexpectedly on September 19, 2019. She had a tremendous impact on my life. She is deeply missed and I take every opportunity I get to acknowledge her as a SHERO. She personified tenacity and dedication.

She was a true athlete and sports person. She and my brother raised two amazing athletes: my niece and nephew. Lynette played women's basketball herself, in high school and on the collegiate level. She later coached women's college basketball at the University of MIchigan - Dearborn and she coached girls' basketball at River Rouge High School. .

Lynette unwittingly was my life coach during our hours of phone conversation and whenever we were together. She demonstrated grace and femininity off the court, and pure power and assertiveness on the court.

Her magnetic and bright light shone in her home life as a wife and mother, her career as a school teacher, daughter, sister, coach and friend. Lynette touched countless lives and helped many of her students and athletes she coached to get on a path of promise. The fruit of her passionate labor, love and compassion continues to germinate across the United States.

Sheba's Jam
A Tribute to Sandra Dobson

In February 2021, I was devastated to learn of Sandra's passing. Two years apart in age, we were Roller Derby League mates. Although we played for different teams (2012/13), Sandra, AKA BADA BOOMZ 4U, saw fit to teach me techniques and made me a much better player/skater. Our closeness in age and being two of four women out of a hundred-women league who were of color, drew us even closer. We had those things in common. With common struggles, we identified on so many levels.

Not only did Sandra educate me in Roller Derby, she taught me a lot about life. She was an unconditional friend who did not criticize me when I set off to do something crazy like packing up my car driving 1200 miles across the country to relocate. Her listening ear and caring heart made me feel so safe, secure and loved. She understood my heartaches and the endless quest for real love.

She was my league mate, prayer partner, confidant, bar stool buddy, rink buddy, diet and fitness accountability partner and advisor. She did all this while being an amazing mother and savvy businesswoman. When we separated geographically, our hearts stayed connected. We chatted a few weeks prior to her passing. She was so full of love, hope and positivity. I hope heaven has a rink so we can catch up as planned for post COVID19.

Sheba's Jam
Introduction

Prima Donna vs.
Prix Madonna

"...being confident of this very thing, that he who began a good work in you will complete it until the day of Jesus Christ." Philippians 1:6

"Now to him who is able to do exceedingly abundantly above all that we ask or think, according to the power that works in us." Ephesians 3:20

During the second quarter of 2012, my life changed pretty dramatically. In April, I got a phone call from my childhood friend, Treva. She talked about putting together a five-star luncheon to honor some amazing women. She would call it: MICHIGAN LEADING LADIES.

She knew who she had in mind for a speaker. A venue had not been chosen yet, nor had the date. She wanted to work it around the Women of Transition monthly prayer gatherings which take place on every first Saturday.

Treva and I began to select women who would be honored. We share ideas about how to make her vision work. I was catching her vision for MLL. She threw out some figures for costs. I sounded like an amazing idea and I wondered how we would really pull it off. Treva was very confident and excited about this endeavor. It would take a couple of days of pondering for me to get on board. I knew that if this thing happened, then truly GOD WOULD HAVE TO DO IT.

My plate was already full, nearly overflowing with a full-time job, a part-time job, three children, writing for several publications, ministry work, and a plethora of other miscellaneous chores and deeds. I was already feeling overwhelmed with life and adding a new thing to my plate, at first seemed unwise.

For me, it was like making a decision to get on a roller coaster. While some people love to ride roller coasters and love the thrill, roller coaster rides make me nervous. The last time I rode a coaster, I remember the anxiety beginning to build as I stood in line. The closer we got to our turn to board, the more nervous I got.

When it was time to hop into the cart, we strapped in and the safety bars were engaged and locked. Once you hear that click, you know there's no turning back. You're in it for the long haul. You're on the ride until it's over. There's no getting off once the ride begins.

This is what my commitment was like to Treva and Leading Ladies. Once I decided to be on board, I was in. No matter how rough the ride, or how many unexpected and abrupt crescents and troughs, I would stay on. I was locked in like, "LET'S DO THIS!!!"

Sheba's Jam

I knew I had to be a part of the Leading Ladies project. Something inside knew this would be a monumental experience. Some of the greatest and most successful things I have done in life were things that I initially felt reluctant about. But when God is in it, no amount of reluctance or reservations can overpower that desire that God puts inside you. God gives us to do His will (Phil.2:13) That feeling that feeds faith trumps fear.

Once the Leading Ladies ball got rolling, I was ready to ride. Anticipation and excitement were high. I was zealous and happy to be a part of this great event. With the actual event being months away, I hoped that the feelings of excitement would remain consistent. Six months of anticipation seemed like a long time to maintain this great feeling.

Fully aware of my personality, I feared that my mood might fluctuate and that my feelings would change. I did not 'want' this to happen, but I knew it was likely. So I was prepared to deal with my passionate emotions, even when they would go against me.

A few weeks in, just as I figured it would happen, I started to feel doubt and an overwhelming fear. "What have I gotten myself into?" Out of nowhere, and for no reason it seems, I started feeling like I made a big mistake. My mind raced, suspicious thoughts began to attack and I felt like I would have a nervous breakdown.

Deep down, I knew this was an attack on my mind

because I had embarked on something amazing. My biggest battles are fought in my mind. I could not sleep. My thoughts were frazzled and I knew I had to pull it together somehow because I was in this thing until the end. Backing out was not an option. I had made a commitment to my friend and to my God and I would not back out no matter what my emotions were doing. I am learning to not allow my emotions to rule my decision making.

I am a highly sensitive person emotionally. This is a gift and a curse. As a gift, it allows me to feel deeply, not only my own feelings, but I can empathize deeply and pick up on the pain and feelings of others. This helps me in my ministry. Adversely, I have a tendency to feel too deeply and I end up overreacting and getting worked up about things more than I should. It takes effort for me to remain balanced. I could feel myself getting off balance.

God is faithful and He knew I needed a diversion. I needed something else to focus on. I needed another cause; another challenge. I needed another trail to blaze. That sounds crazy because I already had plenty of causes, challenges and blazing trails. God has given me this amazing capacity to keep multiple irons in the fire; big irons!

So what would this diversion be? A few weeks prior to my meltdown, I saw a flyer about women's roller derby in Detroit. I didn't even know we had roller derby in Detroit. "How cool is that?" I thought.

Sheba's Jam

I had watched roller derby on television as a child on Saturday mornings. I saw that it was a rough and tough sport for women. What made me most interested in roller derby was that the women were on roller skates. I've been an avid roller skater since I was a year old. I was told that I skated before I walked well. "Your mom put you on skates and when she took the skates off of you, you crawled," a cousin revealed to me.

Both of my parents were roller skaters. In fact, that's how they met. I was raised on roller skates and needless to say, roller skating had become a big part of my life. So any activity involving roller skates would naturally attract me.

As far as the rough and tough part, as a child, I was anything but rough and tough. I was a sweet, gentle, quiet and passive child who was bullied in elementary school. Being rough and tough was a secret desire and fantasy.

I knew I was strong and smart, but my strength was never apparent to others. What could be better than roller derby as a way to skate and show my strong side? What better way to reveal my inner warrior princess? Roller derby would allow me to show the world how strong I really am and it would teach me to fight. I could learn the art of war.

On a flyer I picked up at a coffee shop, I discovered that

SHEBA'S JAM

local tryouts were coming up. By the morning of tryouts, I had already convinced myself that trying out for roller derby was ridiculous. Tryouts were at 9am and when I awoke and glanced at my clock, I realized that my roller derby dream was toast.

Seconds later, I got a text message. The message read: "Good morning derby girl!" The text message was from my friend Ty, to whom I had mentioned the flyer and my wild roller derby dream. For some reason, he believed I could do it.

I hopped out of bed and scurried to get dressed. "I'm going!" I grabbed my skates and was out of the house by 9:20am. I went to the tryouts. I was about 35 minutes late and figured I would take a chance.

When I arrived, they had not started yet. They were still waiting for women to arrive. The building was difficult to find and they wanted to give women a chance to find it. So even though I was late, I was really on time.

I had skates, but no gear. Unfamiliar with the sport currently, I had no idea what to expect or what I should bring. I just showed up with skates. As a result, I could not participate in many of the drills due to safety requirements for equipment. So I watched and listened. On day #2 of tryouts, I had gear and was able to participate.

At age 42, I survived two days of rigorous tryouts and

physical training. Sore in my body, I questioned my sanity wondering if I was too old for such an undertaking. I could barely walk and required assistance putting on my socks and pants. When I realized the younger women were sore too, I felt better. I was also comforted to know that there were other women close to my age playing roller derby. I wasn't so crazy after all.

Meanwhile, I'm in touch with Treva several times a week as we plan for Michigan Leading Ladies! Plans for MLL continue to move forward. We promoted heavily on Facebook. We flooded social media and email and the word spread quickly. People wondered who was backing us and how we had the audacity to pursue such a huge endeavor. We literally stepped out on faith.

Treva provided the design for the first flyer which was a two-sided postcard. When those ran out, I decided to try a different layout. I got a graphic artist to design a new flyer. I provided him with the information and told him to design however he felt led.

When the design was complete, the designer emailed it to me. After some very minor tweaking, the new flyer was a 'go.' One side of the flyer promoted the MLL luncheon and a Friday evening service. The other side promoted the Women of Transition prayer gathering, featuring my photo. The backdrop of the flyer was a checkered flag.

The checkered flag appeared to be taken from a car

race. It blended well with the design, but I couldn't help but wonder: 'why a checkered flag?' What did a race flag have to do with a prayer gathering? Maybe it indicates that we're winning the race? Loving the contrast of black and white, the flyers looked good and we proceeded to pass them out and continue to promote MLL.

After two days of Derby U, I was eligible to try out for roller derby boot camp. I passed the skills test and moved to the next level. Upon completion of an eight week boot camp, I then became eligible to try out for the league. I passed both the skills and written tests. The next step was to participate in a scrimmage.

The scrimmage was public and it was a big deal in the roller derby league community. All the new players were excited about making this far. I played very well in the scrimmage and scored the first ten points. A write-up was done about me in the sports section of my local newspaper, The Telegram. I write for that newspaper and never imagined being written about, especially in the sports section at age 42!

After the scrimmage, I was drafted to a team. I had my eye on a couple of teams because I had gotten to know some of the players. 10 women were in the draft. I waited anxiously for my name to be called by a team. Seven women went before me. Finally, my name was called: Furious Fro Sheba, #407, is drafted to the GRAND PRIX MADONNAS!

Sheba's Jam

I skated over to my new team, my new sisters, my new home. These women embraced me and it felt like a really good fit. I was excited about my new team and just a tad heart-broken about not being a Dame or D-Funk Allstar. However, when I got to know these ladies, I became certain that I was on the right team!

My new team, Grand Prix Madonnas, had cool uniforms. They wore bottoms made of the checker pattern, to represent the flag waved at car races. Tops were purple, like royalty. Grand Prix Madonnas is a play on words mixing the idea of Grand Prix car racing and Prima Donna. I learned that Prima Donna means Leading Lady in Italian!

I started making the connection. I'd been working on Leading Lady stuff for several months. Oh, and the checker flag on the flyer matches our uniforms! Had God been involved in this the whole time?! Remember, I didn't choose the Grand Prix Madonnas. They chose me. I was drafted! There was not a more perfect team for me in the league than the Grand Prix Madonnas also known as GPM!

My team had a reputation of being the 'smart team'! One of my teammates is a lawyer. There is a presidential award-winning scientist who is a professor at the University of Michigan. We have an engineer, a couple of marketing specialists and other professionals. These are not just wild women who hit each other on the derby track. These women are strong, athletic, determined, focused, intelligent and successful in the real world.

Working on Michigan Leading Ladies helped to prepare me for this next step in my life. I learned to push myself beyond what I think are my limits by exercising my faith. Pressing beyond my limitations has crossed over from spiritual to physical. Playing roller derby has taught me to use my physical body in ways I never imagined. My physical endurance now is greater than it was in my 20s and 30s combined. I never thought I would be running, doing push-ups, skating hard, hitting hard, taking hits and falls the way I did. My legs got so strong and my arms got stronger too. This happened because I learned to push myself even when everything in me is screaming 'STOP!'

I have God-confidence and I can do what seems impossible. Working with Treva on MLL, I learned how to work as part of a team. I learned to collaborate with others, merging the use of my gifts and talents with others. Now, play roller derby allows me to continue to develop my ability to be a team player. I learned to be sharpened by team makes, learn from them, disagree with them sometimes, and still remain a team working together. It takes a team to work the dream.

The timing of all this could not have been more perfect. I spent months working with Treva across the country.

Sheba's Jam

MLL had begun to occupy a lot of my time. What would I do when it was over?

Well, as soon as MLL ended, the season for roller derby began! I had a short break in between. I smoothly transitioned from on to another. I began practicing with my team, Grand Prix Madonnas. I immediately began learning valuable lessons in roller derby for everyday life. The derby track is a battleground. I learn to play offensively and defensively. I have to watch my boundaries and play by rules. I learned to hit and take hits. I learned to play in pain, push when I'm tired and face penalties when I break rules. In a sense, I am learning the art of war. Life is a battle and combat skills are essential for survival. Derby has taught me to be strong and courageous! There has not been a dull moment.

I am Janine Folks, known in roller derby as **FURIOUS FRO SHEBA #407**!

Furious means active with great energy and intensity. Passion with zeal.

Fro refers to my hair in its natural state, also known as an afro. I had reverted to my natural hair a year prior to starting roller derby and it is something I am very proud of. I love my natural afro. I embrace and celebrate my Fro. My natural hair journey has been so enlightening and I decided to incorporate the new found beauty and freedom into this experience by making it a part of my

20

Sheba's Jam

derby name.

Sheba, the Queen of Sheba, was very rich, a lover of wisdom and generous. Very wealthy. She is one of my favorite and most admired women of the Bible.

407 for the day I was born.

Establishing an identity for myself, by naming myself, allowed me to take on a new persona pulling together words that are meaningful to me. It made the journey so much more fascinating and fun! I was able to call myself what I decided upon. It was my way of truly identifying myself and who I aim to be.

Sheba's Jam

Inspired by

Roller Derby

SHEBA'S JAM
That's My Jam

Before Roller Derby, a JAM to me, was a song I like. When the beat drops, I yell, "That's my JAM!" I start dancing on the inside and some may or may not spill over to the outside. I love music and rhythmic movement, so jams are very important to me. Jams are the spice of my life.

In the south, a jam often refers to anything that you like or enjoy immensely. Your favorite food is your jam. Your favorite tv show, favorite outfit or whatever brings you joy inside. My favorite song is my jam. When I rock the house on skates, or what some old timers refer to as 'kicking the lights out', we are jamming on roller skates.

Jamming and skating have always gone together for me. With 40+ years of my life spent roller skating, jamming on skates meant jamming to my jams. So when I heard the word jamming, of course, I thought we were going to jam as I knew it.

I came into roller derby knowing how to skate, but I knew absolutely nothing about how the game worked. I had never played or witnessed a modern day bout. All I knew of roller derby is what I saw on television as a child in the 1970's where the women were wild and throwing elbows.

I quickly started learning roller derby lingo and terminology. One of the first things I learned is that my concept of jamming and derby jamming were totally different.

In Roller Derby, jamming is when you are the Jammer. The Jammer is the skater with the star panty on their helmet. It's basically a helmet cover with a star on both sides. The Jammer in roller derby is the one person who can score points when they pass skaters after the first revolution around the track. The Jammer is not only an important position on the track, it requires a high level of skill and stamina. It is a demanding role or position and it can be very rewarding.

I jammed a couple of times and actually scored a few points. I got a chance to show off a little and I also got beat up a little. Another position is a Pivot. The Plvot is on standby in case the Jammer gets tired or for some other reason that strategically beneficial, the Plvot takes the Jammer panty (helmet cover) and takes over the Jam.

The Jammer then becomes a Blocker. The other position. Blockers play offense and defense simultaneously. They help their Jammer score and prevent the opposing Jammer from scoring. I knew absolutely none of this when I showed up to Derby U.

I caught on quickly and if I had found roller derby a little sooner in life, I might have played longer and developed a higher skill level in the sport. Better late than never. I am so happy that I got a chance to experience the culture of Women's Flat Track Roller Derby. It is

SHEBA'S JAM

something that I am very proud of and it was a very rewarding part of my life. Sheba got a chance to JAM! .

SHEBA'S JAM
Victory is Already Won

During my first season of roller derby, as a rookie, I didn't play very much. Still learning the game, I became a good observer and encourager for my team. I guess that was my way of contributing to the team, making myself valuable as I lacked the skill level that experienced veterans had.

My team appreciated my inspirational spirit. Every team needs those reminders that motivate them to be their best. Even though roller derby is a contact sport, a great deal of being a winning team has to do with mental and emotional fitness as much as physical.

My team dominated the track every game. Our first bout was against the championship team. Once we beat them, it seemed like it would be smooth sailing from that point on. However, even though it was a nice confidence booster, we got nervous before each bout as if it were our first.

By our third bout, every team had a vendetta and wanted to beat us. They worked extra hard to take us off of our high horse of being undefeated. While the taste of victory was sweet, instead of getting comfortable, we worked even harder to maintain our position and even excel on all levels.

SHEBA'S JAM

With a perfect track record for our season, we never got arrogant. We tried to get smarter because we knew the other teams wanted to take us down. After practice one day, as we prepared to take on the defending champions, my captain expressed being nervous about the game. We had come so far, the thought of tarnishing our perfect record was quite nerve wrecking. We were all nervous. Then I announced, "WE WILL WIN!! UNDEFEATED CHAMPS!!"

Even though I attempted to assure my team that VICTORY was already ours, that didn't mean we would quit preparing, training and practicing. We would still have to work hard and walk it out. Victory belonged to us already, but we still had to fight to get to it.

I say that to illustrate this: Jesus has promised us VICTORY!!! We who belong to Him, WIN!!! "For everyone who has been born of God overcomes the world. And this is the victory that has overcome the world—our faith" (1 John 5:4 ESV).

Even knowing that the fight is fixed and we win, we still have to prepare and train. We still have to fight. Being guaranteed a win does not mean we stop training and that we don't have to lift a finger to fight. We do. We must continue to exercise and work our faith.

Don't sit and get relaxed and content. We still have to fight the good fight of faith even though the battle is already won. Go. Fight. Win.

Sheba's Jam
Rules

It's probably safe for me to guess, based on my personal observations, that 80% of whether you win or lose in roller derby is based on rules. It is great to be skilled, even highly skilled, but failure to comply with rules makes all the skill in the world vain and of no effect as far as winning.

Rules are designed to maintain order, consistency, boundaries and safety. Even though there are rules and most players are required to know them in order to play, it never fails that during a bout, rules are repeatedly broken and players end up in the penalty box.

There is no guarantee that rules will be followed. Failure to follow rules results in penalty. The consequence of penalty is a set back and should act as a deterrent to future rule violations. Nevertheless, rules still get broken.

We are given rules in life. For the Christian, these rules are found in the Bible. Even though we read the rules, we study the rules, and try to adhere to them, it is inevitable that at some point, on some level, we violate the rules. The Bible even tells us, "For all have sinned and fall short of the glory of God" (Romans 3:3).

Even when we think we are following the rules to a T, we cannot keep ourselves blemish free. "All of us have become like one who is unclean, and all our righteous acts are like filthy rags..." (Isaiah 64:6). Rules get broken.

SHEBA'S JAM

Period.

The Lord said, "My grace is sufficient for you, for my power is made perfect in weakness. Therefore I will boast all the more gladly about my weaknesses, so that Christ's power may rest on me" (2 Corinthians 12:9).

If it were humanly possible to live life without breaking a rule (Bible), there would be no need for the blood of Jesus Christ. There would be no need for grace. Even though there are penalties for sin and breaking rules, or consequences, God is still gracious. He will forgive us if we confess (I John 1:9).

Follow the rules. Do the best you can as much as it lies within you. If, or should I say when, you mess up, there may be a penalty, but repent. May the grace of God be with you and keep you.

SHEBA'S JAM
Strong & Courageous

Someone asked me regarding roller derby: "Aren't you afraid you'll get hurt?"

I replied, "No. If you're in fear, you might as well stay off the track."

You cannot play roller derby effectively if you are afraid and consumed with fear. Fear clouds your thinking. I am fully aware of the risks and potential dangers. I have witnessed women get major and minor injuries. I have seen women in pain. I have fallen and have been in pain. But none of that has deterred my zeal for the game of derby.

Before I play, I always pray for God's protection. Then I play smart. I stay on guard to protect myself. At the same time, I move forward. Fearlessly, I play to win.

The more I play roller derby, the more I see how it parallels life. You cannot win when your mind is always on the possibility of losing. When I teach beginning skaters, I cannot teach them if they are terrified. They clinch up so badly, they cannot move without feeling support. On the opposite end, an overconfident person who lacks skill will hurt themselves. A skater has to have the right balance of caution and zeal. This is required in real life.

You cannot live fully if you're afraid. God did not give us

the spirit of fear and timidity (I Tim. 1:7). Refuse to adopt fear. It does not belong to you. Get rid of the fear. Instead, hold on to this: God gave us a spirit of power, of love and self-discipline [sound mind/good judgment] (I Timothy 1:7). Use it!

Pray for wisdom daily. God said He'd give it generously if we ask (James 1:5). If you're living in Godly wisdom, there is no need to be afraid. God says He will hold your right hand, saying unto you, Fear not; I will help you." (Isa. 41:13)

When Moses was preparing Joshua to go to the promised land in Joshua 1, he knew there would be many challenges ahead to tempt them to turn back and run. He knew there would be things that could cause fear and fear is paralyzing. So Moses charged them repeatedly: BE STRONG AND COURAGEOUS!!

Sheba's Jam
Gaps

I'm working on a book about what roller derby taught me and principles it reinforced. There are so many analogies I have gleaned playing this game/sport. I think all athletes are exceptional people because they have to exercise physical and mental discipline, strategize and continuously hone their craft to obtain and maintain their A game. Their competitive nature keeps them sharp.

This is how we should live. After all, life is like a race. The Apostle Paul reflected on how he had run his race (2 Timothy 4.7). We don't play games with life, but the analogy can be made to a game, and we are the players, trying to win. The ultimate prize is to hear those precious words when we leave this life and enter God's presence: Well done my good and faithful servant! (Matt. 25.21)

Now you don't have to be an athlete to think like one. You can train your mind to think competitively and be disciplined. You have to be a keen observer.

Playing roller derby, an important component to the game was 'finding gaps.' Particularly for the jammer, the skater who can score points, this is important. When a jammer or skater needs to get through the pack or penetrate a wall (a group of skaters trying to prevent an opponent from passing), she looks for gaps.

Sheba's Jam

She seeks an opening that she can penetrate so she can get through. If she remains trapped or behind the pack, she cannot score. Her objective is to get through. She is constantly maneuvering and looking for openings. When she sees one, she takes it by force.

She moves quickly to get through. She might even appear passive for a moment and then jet through. She may juke to fake opponents out to make a hole for herself to pass through. Sometimes holes are open and she has to see them in order to take advantage of them.

In life, we can find ourselves in some tight spots. Situations that we cannot seem to be able to penetrate through. Recall 1 Corinthians which says, "...when you are tempted, He (God) will make a way of escape..."

God is the best at making escape opportunities when He needs to deliver you. Sometimes, you can be creative yourself, with God's guidance of course, and make openings to get out of a mess so you can score.

The key to it is, being alert and watchful. We must always pay attention to what's happening and what God is doing. If we have our heads down in despair, we might miss the opening. If we don't press hard, we might passively forfeit our escape. Keep your eyes open and watch for those gaps. Get out of that bondage.

Sheba's Jam
Hit & Run

I remember the first time I received a full blown hit in roller derby. I was blindsided and couldn't believe how fast I was swept off my feet. I was skating one minute and the next thing I knew I was on the ground looking up, like: "Ouch. Who did that?"

I collected myself and got up literally feeling a little disoriented. That's when I realized that I really hate falling.
Not wanting to fall like that again, I made it a goal to learn how to handle hits. I knew there would be times I'd fall, but I wanted to avoid them as much as possible.

Practicing with my team helped me learn how to handle hits. First of all, you need to be aware so that a hit does not catch you off guard, by surprise. You should always see a hit coming.

When you see a hit coming, you can do one of three things: Absorb, counter or avoid the hit with a juke move. When you absorb a hit, you just take it and try to remain sturdy on your feet.

You can counter the hit by hitting back when you see it coming. It's counter action where you impact the hitter, deflecting the impact back onto the one who is hitting you. Oftentimes the hitter goes down instead of the target. In other words, you can make a hitter's hit backfire on them.

Sheba's Jam

The other thing you can do is try to avoid the hit altogether by making the hitter miss. You do this by quickly getting out of the path of the hitter with a quick juke move. The hitter will miss you and possibly go out of bounds. This is good for you and bad for them.

In life, we take hits. The worst hits are the ones that catch you off guard and knock you down. The devil is like the hitter who is trying to take you out. The devil wants you down on the ground, disabled, so he can score.

If you don't see the devil coming, he'll blind side you. This is why the Bible tells us to be 'wide awake and sober' (1 Thes. 5.6) and to 'beware of dogs' (Phil. 3.2).

We need to be aware of where the devil is and see him coming. You cannot be distracted or not paying attention. Your mind has to be right. When you recognize him coming, you need to react appropriately.

You can brace yourself and take the hit and refuse to go down. You can counter the action and redirect it back to the devil. The devil will get a black eye trying to give you one. You can avoid the hit by simply getting out of the way. You have to be quick, agile and have great timing.

Watch and pray. Handle those hits! Don't let them handle you. Don't be a hit and run victim. Don't let the enemy sneak or ease in on you. Watch and pray.

SHEBA'S JAM
Drills

Sometimes people complain about something being drilled into their head. What they don't realize is that sometimes it takes doing and hearing something over and over again for it to become a part of the fabric of our being. Practicing something repeatedly makes that thing become second nature like a reflex that you do without even thinking about it.

This is what drills do. In roller derby, we practice drills again and again. Doing something once does not give you mastery over a skill. We can be gifted at many things, but practice hones our craft. Even when we have perfected something, we can lose the skill and become less effective if we fail to practice and do drills to reinforce the knowledge and skill.

Just the same, we read the same Bible over and over again. We need to drill the Word of God into our heads repeatedly. We go to church again and again. Bible study is something we routinely need to do and we go through the motions of studying. This is the only way to get the Word ingrained in us. This is how we make God's Word a part of our being.

Some drills are moderate and others are intense. Nevertheless, we need drills in our lives to reinforce what we are learning as well as what we have mastered. It's like doing maintenance. It never stops. As long as we are participating in this activity called life, we need to repeat and practice the drill of studying God's Word and communicating with Him in prayer. Don't complain about the drills. It will make the appropriate responses to challenges become second nature and we will do what we need to do without putting too much thought into it.

That's why it's so important to read scriptures over and over again. That's why we go to church week after week; Bible study week after week. We fellowship week after week and day after day. This repetition should never get old but instead, it should be perfecting us and perfecting our faith. If we do these things repeatedly and don't get better at it, we have to ask ourselves if we are really paying attention and really disciplining ourselves to improve and make excellence second nature.

We only get better at the things we practice. There is a reason this verse is in the Bible: "Make every effort to present yourself approved to God, a worker having no need to be ashamed, guiding the word of truth along a straight path (2 Tim. 2.15 LEB)." The KJV uses the word "study." Study God's Word, study life, study people, study situations, and study everything around you. Seek God. Learn and grow. Pray as you and your faith are perfected day by day.

SHEBA'S JAM
Swivel

When I talk to people about roller derby, I often relate it to life. I often talk about how it has taught me to live more strategically and has increased my ability to be aware. For survival and success, we must always be aware of our surroundings, what's coming and what's going.

A crucial thing in roller derby is to keep your head on a swivel, pivoting frequently. You have to be aware of what's in front of you and what's behind you all at the same time. You look ahead to see where you're going and how you will maneuver. You also have to know what's behind you and trying to sneak up on you.

If you look ahead for too long without looking back, you will be in trouble. If you look back for too long without seeing and knowing what's in front of you, you will be in trouble. So it's a constant swivel of looking ahead and back. Awareness is vital.

In life, we have to look ahead and keep our eyes on the prize. We look to our future with great anticipation and we maneuver through life's challenges and obstacles. We see footstools ahead and use them to stand on. All the while, we are aware of and affected by things we learned and experienced in the past. Sometimes ugly events or hurtful memories of the past try to creep and sneak up on us to get us down and we need to see those things coming.

We also need to look back sometimes so that we can remember the great and wonderful things God has done for us to remind us of the glory to come as we look ahead. Keeping our heads on a swivel enables us to be aware, coming and going. Like the Bible says, "Be vigilant..." (Mark 13:37).

Sheba's Jam
Catch That Whip

I recently began learning and playing women's roller derby. I realized quickly that roller derby is not just a bunch of women hitting each other on roller skates. There is a method to the madness requiring skill, technique and strategy.

Roller derby mirrors my real life. There's a lot of falling and getting back up, getting knocked down again, breaking through barriers, avoiding obstacles, watching and maneuvering, moving things out of the way, hitting, racing forward to score, fatigue, struggling and pressing with all my might. There are rules that you see frequently being broken. You endure and persevere.

Some lives may be like skating in the park, free from resistance and roughness. My life is more like roller derby. It's more like a battlefield. Nevertheless, one thing I know for sure in my life is that I have the victory due to my affiliation with Jesus Christ (1 Cor. 15:57).

Successful roller derby requires excellent communication. You always have to be aware of what's happening on the track. Know where your teammates are as well as your opponents. Keep your opponent from scoring while helping your own team to score.

Look out for your team mates. If you see a teammate struggling, in need of a boost, and you're in a position to do so, you give them a 'whip.' In derby, a 'whip' is where you grab a distressed team mate to push or pull them. A transfer of power and speed takes place. It's like a supercharger from a friend.

When life gets rough, a 'whip' of encouragement may be in order. A life 'whip' helps a person in distress go forward, providing strength for the journey. It can be a hug, an 'I love you,' presence, a listening ear, or simply a caring heart that spends time. A whip can be an uplifting Bible verse or an empowering sermon. A whip is a helping hand.

Sometimes you need to 'whip' it. Sometimes you need to catch that 'whip.' The Bible says: "...Encourage one another and build each other up (1 Thes. 5:11). Encourage one another daily" (Heb. 3:13).

SHEBA'S JAM
Referee

I was watching some boxing footage. I watched the fighters relentlessly go at each other. Punch after punch. Giving it and taking it, all while bouncing around the ring continuously. (Keep in mind similar principles apply in roller derby as well).

I thought about how exhausting it could be. I also thought about how on point you have to be in order to be a successful boxer. Your endurance has to be up to par as well as mastery of skill and mental stamina. During a boxing match, our attention is usually focused on the boxers.

I started paying attention to the referee. I watched how he also bounced around right along with the boxers. He stayed close enough so that he could monitor the boxers, but at just enough distance to stay out of their way. The ref watches every move, observes that rules are being followed and breaks the fighters up when they become entangled with each other.

What I noticed about the ref is that he has to be in as good of shape as the boxers, almost. He is not punching or being punched, but his endurance level has to be up there with the fighters. He cannot miss a beat. He cannot slack on his attentiveness to everything going on between the boxers.

Watching the referee, I likened his role to that of a

parent, a shepherd, guardian or leader in general. You have to monitor everything. You don't always intervene, but you watch closely. You have to keep up with what's going on and it can get tiring. You have to know the rules and make sure they are being followed. You have to intervene when things get messy and clear it up. It's a demanding job.

When those they lead are going at it fiercely, the ref has to be right in there with them, in the midst of the madness. The ref has to have good discernment to know when and when not to break something up. The ref has to know how to stay out of the way and let them do what they do. It's a delicate balance that requires wisdom, skill and endurance.

The ref is a respected figure in the game. What the ref says is gospel and not to be argued with by boxers. The ref makes the calls. It can be argued, but generally, what the referee says, usually goes.

In life, sometimes you may feel like a referee. As a leader, parent, supervisor, guardian, guide, chaperon, teacher, mentor or anytime you are responsible or appointed over people. This is a huge responsibility and the weight of it is heavy. Your choices in making calls affect how the game goes. People are counting on you to do well.

The boxers [players] and the referee have to know the rules in the ring and on the court. In life, we have to know the rules. Our rules come from the Word of God. The ref insures that rules are followed and have to watch. But first, the ref has to know the rules in order to enforce them.

Remember this: "All Scripture is given by inspiration of God, and is profitable for doctrine, for the reproof, for correction, for instruction in righteousness, that the people of God may be complete, thoroughly equipped for every good work" [2 Tim. 3.16,17].

Sometimes I feel like God is a referee in my life too. He stands back enough for me to do what I need to do, based on what I've learned and trained for. But when necessary, He steps in to make sure I'm not violated or hurt. Thank you Lord.

Sheba's Jam
Iron Sharpens Iron

When I think of iron sharpening iron, I imagine sparks flying and sounds of metal pounding fiercely. Grinding resistance causes iron to be sharpened. Its sound is loud and unpleasant. It's rough.

Iron sharpening is not a gentle or quiet process. It takes hard hitting to sharpen edges. A gentle process would leave an iron dull.

So when we read, "As iron sharpens iron, so does a friend sharpen the countenance of a friend," (Prov. 27:17) should we expect an easy pleasant process?

While we expect and desire friends to love us unconditionally, we must also realize that sparks will sometimes fly. Unless friends challenge you, they cannot sharpen you. We will take hits from those within our own camp. I call it productive friction.

Hits we take from our friends strengthen us to handle the hits that come from our enemies. We cannot take these hits personal and hate our friends for it. We have to learn the benefit and blessing of sparring.

Boxers know this. Boxers have sparring partners who hit them to strengthen them for their real fights. In roller derby, teammates hit and take hits from each other to prepare them for their 'real' opponents. None of this is taken personally. In fact, it's frowned upon if you are too delicate. A real friend wants to make you strong. Too many of us get offended when we should be gleaning strength.

As a parent, I had to be hard on my daughter sometimes. She interpreted as me attacking her. I explained that if she could not take it from me, how will she take it from the real world? The real world

Those who have never had to fight get a rude awakening when they are finally faced with a fight. We have to learn how to fight and our training begins within our own circle. If we are not teaching our children how to handle conflict by having conflict, we are not serving them. Constant peace and harmony does not challenge us. Smooth sailing does not toughen our skin. I'm not advocating turmoil, but we need to be challenged to be sharpened sometimes.

Don't get all offended by internal battles. When you face battles within your camp, among friends, don't necessarily lose the friendship, unless you really feel led to. Use those interactions as lessons to prepare you and strengthen you for battles with your real enemies. Even when 'real' enemies are inside your camp masquerading as friends, God can use those situations for your good also, to teach you. Remember, getting your iron sharpened will not always be a pretty process. You will be challenged and it should be done with love (not abuse).

SHEBA'S JAM
Front and Back

In roller derby, it is very important to be aware of your surroundings. You need to be aware of what is happening in front of you as well as behind you, at the same time. Too much attention to one or the other can cause problems. Skaters must learn proper and effective balance. Otherwise, you won't be an effective player.

In life, we have to look ahead and remember the past, at the same time. My father often would say to me, "History is your best teacher." We have to remember the things our past has taught us, which requires looking back. Just like David did when he faced the giant, Goliath. He remembered how God had empowered him to kill a lion and a bear (I Samuel 17:36). This was his motivation to believe that God would help again to kill what was in front of him, Goliath.

We look back not only at our past, but we look behind us to see what is coming up on us. We look ahead to see where we need to go and we look ahead to follow the path in front of us. "Let your eyes look straight ahead, and your eyelids look right before you" (Proverb 4:25). Being aware of what is ahead as well as what is behind, takes a keen sense of vision and discernment.

In roller derby, sense there aren't eyes in the back of our heads, we often had to pivot or swivel our head and body, we had to do quick turns, use our 'feelers', peripheral vision and all of our senses to be aware of what's coming and going. We had to learn how to use other senses in addition to our eyes, in order to be fully aware.

Sometimes we can sense things without actually looking at them. If you're really in tune with what is happening around you, you will be able to recall what you need to know and have some foresight. This ability helps us in life. Too much of any one thing can go bad. Too much dwelling on what's behind can cause you to run into a problem, literally. Only looking ahead can do the same thing because you have to draw on past experience in order to use knowledge.

We can tap into a supernatural ability to be aware of everything in our sphere. We have to do this in life. It's a survival technique. A technique for successful living. Knowing how to balance our attention on the front and back. But one thing that is for sure, in derby and in life, whether you are looking in front of you or looking behind you, you must ROLL FORWARD. Sometimes we take steps back, but not too far back. We have to keep it moving in the forward direction.

Sheba's Jam
Knee Pads

Some people do not try things because they are afraid of falling. People don't like to fall, because usually, falling hurts. It's embarrassing and you could possibly get injured. So it's no wonder why people are paralyzed by this fear of falling.

There is much territory uncharted, dreams unfulfilled, and full potential not realized due to the fear of falling. The fear of falling makes me think back to when I played roller derby.

As an official rule, we were not allowed on the track to play unless we had on full gear, in addition to our skates. This included knee pads, as well as a helmet, elbow pads, mouth guard, and wrist guard. Falling is inevitable in roller derby. It's going to happen. But the thing is, you have to protect yourself and we did that by wearing our gear. Knee pads would not stop us from falling, but it would cushion the knees to absorb the impact and keep you protected.
I remember getting hit one time and I knew I was going down.

I could not avoid this fall that I knew was coming. Therefore, knowing I was about to fall, the best thing I could do was fall well. I knew my knee pads were on, so I made sure I landed properly on my knees and it wouldn't hurt me. Without the knee pads, my knees would've been completely crushed. But I knew my protective gear was under me, so I didn't worry.

Sometimes in life, we see ourselves about to fall. But when we are geared up properly, there is no need to fear. Just like there's the rule that you cannot play roller derby if you don't have on your gear, in life we should be required to put gear on. The whole armor of God!

"Put on the whole armor of God, that ye may be able to stand against the wiles of the devil (Eph 6.11)."

"...having girded your waist with truth, having put on the breastplate of righteousness, and having shod your feet with the preparation of the gospel of peace; above all, taking the shield of faith with which you will be able to quench all the fiery darts of the wicked one. And take the helmet of salvation, and the sword of the Spirit, which is the word of God; praying always with all prayer and supplication in the Spirit, (v.14-18)."

If we do this, we don't have to live in fear. We don't have to be afraid to follow our dreams and fulfill our destiny. We won't be afraid to leave our comfort zone because we know God has us covered. If we fall, He will be there because we are in relationship with Him. Always put on your gear and the idea of falling will not terrify you.

Take that attitude with you!! Time is short! Time out for being too afraid to do what you know you need to do. Tighten up your relationship with God and KNOW that He alone has you covered!! "He will cover you with his feathers, and under his wings you will find refuge; his

Sheba's Jam

faithfulness will be your shield and rampart (Psa 91.4)." Make it amazing!! God is with you!!

"Now unto him that is able to keep you from falling, and to present you faultless before the presence of his glory with exceeding joy (Jude 24)."

Sheba's Jam
Endurance

The thing about roller skating is, it's a cardiovascular activity. To be good at skating, your heart and lungs have to be in good condition. Your legs can be strong, but if your heart and lungs are not strong, you will not last long on the skate floor. You will get tired, short of breath and probably want to sit down.

The more you skate, the better your endurance gets. Every skater likes to maintain optimal endurance. Endurance is the ability to do something difficult for a long time. Skating is not something you just do for a few minutes and stop. Skating is an activity that is performed typically for about two hours.

If you skate regularly, you maintain endurance. In as little as a week, if you stop skating, you can lose endurance. If you take a break from skating, you will feel it when you return because your endurance will not be the same. You will be more tired than prior to the break.

Breaks are good for rest and restoration, but if a break is too long, it can cause setbacks. Well, the same thing happens in our spiritual life. We need endurance. Endurance, our ability to have stamina, staying power, persistence to survive and thrive, depends on how consistently we exercise in spiritual things.

We have to maintain our relationship with God. We do that through prayer and making the scriptures a part of our being, by reading them. Regular godly fellowship also feeds our spirit for endurance. Long breaks can set us back. The Bible makes it clear that we need endurance.

"For you have need of endurance, so that after you have done the will of God, you may receive the promise (Hebrew 10:36 NKJV)."

"Therefore we also, since we are surrounded by so great a cloud of witnesses, let us lay aside every weight, and the sin which so easily ensnares us, and let us run with endurance the race that is set before us (Hebrews 12:1 NKJV)."

Be mindful of your spiritual endurance. Keep at it and invest the time. It will bless your life.

SHEBA'S JAM
Uniforms

When you're playing a team sport or a part of an organization, people need to be able to identify you as a part of the team. My roller derby team wore purple and black & white checkers. It was our trademark. We integrated it into almost everything and it became a part of our identity.

In order for a game to be played effectively, teammates wear uniforms. This allows you to easily identify your teammates for support and you can easily spot your opponents. Without uniforms, there would be lots of confusion and probably pandemonium.

In society, we often assess people by their uniform. But since people generally don't wear uniforms as normal attire, we judge by outer appearances. Whether intentional or not, consciously or not, we tend to make some determinations about people based on what they are wearing.

We also assess according to behaviors and other obvious attributes. What kind of message are you conveying? According to your own persona and attire, whose team are you identifying with? What does it make people think about you?

We often say we don't care what people think about us. But whether we care or not, some people notice, and sometimes it matters. This is why for the most part, you wouldn't wear dirty smelly clothes to a job interview or celebratory event. Generally, we try to dress for the occasion we are attending.

In the Bible, I imagine that soldiers who fought in armies wore similar armor designs and colors. This would have helped them to know who to kill and who not to kill. Other than that implication, the Bible does not speak on uniform wearing.

However, the Bible does tell us how we can recognize each other: "You can identify them by their fruit, that is, by the way they act. Can you pick grapes from thorn bushes, or figs from thistles? A good tree produces good fruit, and a bad tree produces bad fruit. A good tree can't produce bad fruit, and a bad tree can't produce good fruit (Matthew 7:16-18NLT). This was pointed out because 'false prophets were coming disguised as harmless sheep but are really vicious wolves.' They were told to beware (v.15).

With that in mind, mind your fruit. It's your uniform so to speak. Uniforms are a sign of solidarity and cohesion. Be mindful of who and what you are representing. What's your uniform?

SHEBA'S JAM
Teamwork

I've heard it said many times: "Teamwork makes the dream work." Some things can only get done when you have a great group of people working together. Playing roller derby, teamwork was a key element. Without it, you cannot win.

When you're taking on a major task, however, first things first. First you pray. After you pray, you pause a bit and connect so that you can sense promptings and directives from on high. Pray for favor, strength, courage, provision and protection.

Your team will come together. Everyone on the team has strengths and weaknesses. As a team with various talents and gifts, use them all to the advantage of the team. Use them constructively and strategically for optimal results.
When I was in college, we learned about something called 'synergy.'

Synergy is simply cooperation, collaboration or the combined effect of working together. We also learned a concept called 'groupthink,' which is basically, conformity to group values. These things are helpful when it comes to teamwork. It gets everyone on one accord with a common goal.

How good and pleasant it is we dwell together in unity (Psalm 133:1).

Sheba's Jam

We all have gifts. Not the same gift necessarily, but we have gifts. Collectively we use our gifts for a common purpose. As we learn in I Corinthians 12. There are many members (or parts), but we function in the same body (group/team).

Nehemiah could have never rebuilt the walls of Jerusalem without a group of people, each doing their part, in their place according to their level and area of expertise. It really does take teamwork to make the dream work. Our individual work is important. Our work as a team member is important as well. Don't neglect either one. Be sure to do your part. God bless you.

SHEBA'S JAM
Knocked Silly

Usually, the intent behind hitting someone, is to knock them out, or at least disable them. When I played roller derby, one of my teammates had that phrase in her name. In the game of roller derby, knocking someone silly gets them out of your way and makes it easier for your jammer to score.

I never really knew what knocked silly meant until it happened to me. If you don't get knocked out cold, being knocked silly causes you to feel disoriented and you have to regain your footing. This could take a few seconds.

In roller derby, even a split second can change an entire outcome. Every moment counts because timing is everything. Any amount of time spent knocked silly, gives your opponent an advantage. For that moment, you become a non-factor, because you are ineffective in that state.

In life, things happen to us that completely knock us silly. We become stunned and momentarily unable to function. Feeling disoriented, confused, mixed-up, thrown off, even perplexed! You are forced to stop because in that moment, you're not even sure where you're going or why.

Getting knocked silly in life isn't about getting physically hit. Traumatic events, disappointments, broken heartedness, prolonged sadness, emotional pain, being abused, being victimized and other catastrophic or even seemingly minor events can knock our minds silly.

When that happens, however it happens, you have to get your equilibrium back. Regain your balance and composure. Get back oriented to who you are, where you are and what time it is. Get your mind right and you can resume movement. Otherwise, you might go the wrong way and mess up.

Once you pull it together, with God's help of course, and by His grace, you can think clearly again. We have to take charge of our thoughts (2 Cor. 10.5).

When we come back to our senses, we can return to where we belong, just like the lost son in Luke 11:17. Yes, we can get knocked silly in life, but thank God we don't have to stay silly. We can get ourselves together and reclaim our lives!

Sheba's Jam
The Pack

In roller derby, there's a thing called 'the pack.' The pack is the range of space where skaters/players can legally skate and be considered 'in play'. The pack is a cluster of skaters from both teams and you cannot go ten feet ahead or behind. If you do, you are considered, 'out of play' and you are penalized. These skaters are blockers (8). The 2 jammers, the ones who can go around the track to score, are the only exception to the pack rule because they have a different responsibility and role.

So you have to maintain the speed of the pack and stay within ten feet. You're only a valid player if you stay within the designated range, in the pack. You have to be able to stay with the speed of the pack, which means you are constantly gauging your pace. You can't go too fast and you can't fall too far behind.

In life, we must learn to gauge our pace. This means we have to have self-awareness. The 'pack' can be anything. It can be something that's important to us. For example, let's say that the 'pack' is our goal. We have to keep our eyes on our goals and be careful to stay within reach of them. We cannot go too far ahead and we cannot fall behind them.

If the 'pack' is our family, we have to be watchful of what is going on and stay within a good reach in order to be effective. If the 'pack' is our relationship with God, we have to keep our eyes on it and make sure that within the sphere of where God wants us to be. We cannot leave God by going too fast. We cannot fall behind by not moving at a fast enough pace. It's a continuous monitoring of what we are doing and where we are.

It's a constant speeding up and slowing down just to stay within the realm of where we need to be. It requires attention and focus. This is not something you can half-heartedly do. It's not a side-hobby or spare time thing. It is important and we must stay in proper range, lest we end up 'out of play' and in the 'penalty box.'

Our goal should be to stay within the will of God. We learn about the will of God by reading His Word, praying, and listening when He speaks to our heart. When we follow what we know to be right, it keeps us in the right place. If we are out of place, we are totally ineffective, and that could cause consequences (penalty).

"Watch and pray, so that you may not enter into temptation" (Mark 14:38). Temptation tries to lure you from the pack. "...press toward the mark for the prize of the high calling of God in Christ Jesus" (Phil. 3:14).

SHEBA'S JAM
Strong Arms

When I went to a roller derby orientation program, I thought I was just going to learn about roller derby. I didn't know we were going to get physical. I had no idea I would realize how important arms are and why they need to be strong.

After going around talking about our skating background, we went to the middle of the floor. We were told to wear gym clothes and gym shoes, but I had no idea what was in store for me physically. I just wanted to skate. That was easy for me.

So we line up and we start jogging. Not my favorite thing to do, but I hung in there. If that wasn't enough, we did other jumping type exercises. I thought I was in shape because I was a skater. This was a startling reminder of how bad my endurance was.

We got to the part where we had to drop down and plank and do push ups. "Are you kidding me? I am here to skate, not be an Olympian!" My arm strength was nil as I struggled to hold up my body with my arms. "OMG! My arms are so weak!" I realized. Trembling at my attempt to hold up, I thought they were going to kick me out. The other women were holding up like they've done this all their lives. They were strong!

Well, I hung in there, amazingly! Literally two hours of exercising. I didn't think I had it in my 42 year old body. I couldn't even do this stuff in my 20s or 30s! I hadn't even tried.

The next day, I was terribly sore, but I went back for more! It comforted me to see that the younger women were also sore from the previous day of physical training. "So it's not just that I'm older. Whew."

I proceeded and passed skills testing to move on to the boot camp for eight weeks. My body must have thought I had lost my mind. I went through the sore legs and then sore arms.

My arms were so sore, I could barely lift anything and carrying out daily functions was a great challenge. My arms were in excruciating pain, to the point I went to the doctor to see if it was serious. Muscles and tendons just needed to heal.

I developed the ability to plank, holding up my body weight with my arms! Instead of slowing down with age, I actually got faster and stronger. When I think about my arms getting stronger, I cannot help but think about the Virtuous Woman of Proverbs 31.

In verse 17, it says, "She...strengthens her arms." In addition to being Godly, ingenious, resourceful, a business woman, an amazing mother, a loving wife and over all phenomenal femme, she also saw fit to strengthen her arms!

Not just to look fabulous, but so she could be strong. I'm sure lifting to perform daily functions for her work and

Sheba's Jam

life with endurance helped her to be more productive and effective. Warriors need strong arms.

In addition, this woman of virtue could spiritually lift others with her wisdom, encouragement and inspiration!! Find your strength!!! It's inside you. Strengthen your arms!! Strike the "I am woman" pose, hold your arm up with fist balled and make a muscle!

Sheba's Jam
Reward

One of the questions I was asked often when I played roller derby was, "Do you get paid to play?"
The answer was, "no.'

To my knowledge, most women who play roller derby do not get paid. But when you see them play with so much heart and soul, I can see why people would think derby girls get paid to skate and play. Actually, for me, it was quite the opposite.

Your heart really has to be in it, or you will not last long. There is a lot of investment and sacrifice. We had to pay dues to cover practice venues and time. We had to buy skates and equipment and keep it updated. The sport can be expensive and skaters love it so much, that playing actually costs and they are more than willing to pay. In roller derby, the payoff was not in money, but other things that are worth more than a dollar amount.

Every skater has a unique reason and purpose for participating and personal rewards vary. For me, the priceless things I experienced were: exhilaration, great workouts, a sense of belonging (team), sisterhood, a challenge, personal empowerment, fun, laughter, growth, surpassing my perceived limits, a sense of accomplishment, ability to be competitive, learning new skills, using critical thinking skills, testing your own strength, increasing your strength mentally and physically and so much more. I could go on, but this partial list gives you an idea of the rewards of playing roller derby.

Just like any other hobby, people do these things for the love of it and how it makes them feel. The fulfillment that the hobby brings is the reward, even if they have to make sacrifices and investments. People who love their hobbies and pastimes usually participate in them with zeal and enthusiasm! They do it for the love of it.

Wouldn't it be great if we could translate the same enthusiasm over into our vocations and workplaces? Some have accomplished this and others are trying. If we can see what we do as a blessing and in some way beneficial, we can learn to value what we do. Let us learn to see the blessings that outweigh the sacrifices. If this is not happening, then we need to re-evaluate what we are doing and why?

Make adjustments and move toward doing things you can be passionate about and actually look forward to doing them. Dealing with 'people' is inevitable and sometimes that makes our tasks challenging, but we must learn to rise above it, foster good working relationships and learn to enjoy what we are doing.

SHEBA'S JAM

Rewards can be financial, but there are some rewards that are worth more than money. With all our needs being met, we want to experience the things and the work that bring us the utmost joy. When we accomplish this, we can find our work and what we are doing gratifying and satisfying. Then it will be much easier for us to follow Colossian 3:32-24: "Whatever you do, do it heartily, as to the Lord, and not unto people; Knowing that of the Lord you shall receive the reward of the inheritance: for you serve the Lord Christ." This is your reward.

SHEBA'S JAM
Falling

When I teach children how to roller-skate, their biggest fear is falling. As they wobble and teeter they look desperately for me to keep them in the upright position. Unable to balance, they are excited and horrified as they take on this new task.

The best roller-skating student is the one who is fearless. Not cocky or overconfident, but one who is not afraid to fall. When you are a beginner, falling is expected. You fall, get up, and try again. Repeat.

"I don't want to get hurt," is the biggest complaint.

In life, some of us are afraid to fall when we are learning something new. Learning a new thing takes us out of our comfort zone. We don't flow, we stumble clumsily. Like the beginning skater, we have to find our equilibrium and balance. Take it easy. Don't expect to become an expert overnight. We have to connect with the environment and learn the ropes, like the skater who connects their feet to the floor and becomes one. It's a process and we need to allow ourselves time.

When (not if) we fall, we have to fall strategically, if at all possible. Attempting to break the fall can make matters worse. Falling is a part of learning. It may hurt, but we recover and resume.

Sheba's Jam

So why do we beat ourselves up so badly when we fall? God is not shocked or surprised. He expects it in spite of our best intentions. Like Peter (in Matthew 26), who swore he'd never deny Christ, we desire to be capable of being invincible without faithfulness. But there are things inside us that we don't even realize are there until unexpected circumstances arise; things that trip us. We avoid it as much as possible by taking our time and being cautious, but even the best of the best fall sometimes. Even expert roller-skaters are not exempt from falling.

There is no need to deem ourselves failures when we fall. Some of the most successful people I know have fallen repeatedly. Even Peter, who denied Christ after swearing not to, went on to have a powerful ministry to where people were healed simply by encountering his shadow (Acts 5:15,16). What if he had written himself off due to his fall? Instead, he repented, got back up and kept it moving.

No need in wallowing in the pity of our falls. Repent. Realign your thoughts and get back in the game. Falling comes with life. The higher you are, the harder the fall, but don't stay down. A just man falls seven times and rises again (Prov. 26:14).

Even when we fear falling, let us remember that "HE is able to keep you from falling, and to present you faultless before the presence of his glory with exceeding joy, to the only wise God our Savior, be glory and majesty, dominion and power, both now and ever. Amen (Jude 25). Don't go throwing yourself to the ground, but don't stop living because you are afraid of falling. Follow the Son.

SHEBA'S JAM
Derby Changed Me

If I took the time to write all the ways derby affected my life, I don't think you would have the attention span to read it all. Maybe I am underestimating you! Anyway, I decided to sum up a few things here as I close this segment of Sheba's Jam.

Attending Derby U was a great decision that I almost did not make. It's amazing how life goes and how we can be directed and redirected all while unaware. My life was enhanced by this crazy wild game. I got to do things that I had only done as a child and never thought I would do again, like relay races on skates, play tag, and other unconventional games, laughing and screaming wildly. I did things the 40 something year old hospice and hospital chaplain could not do in regular life.

I got to moonlight and LIVE!

I met so many beautiful women from all kinds of backgrounds and various professions. There were 100 of us in the league, plus other leagues we networked with. It is a subculture.

I learned love on a new level, an unconditional level. The common bond of loving the game of roller derby, united women who may have never met or connected otherwise. Not only did we connect, we bonded and united, functioning as a unit on the track.

SHEBA'S JAM

Even though we were compliant with league rules and practiced the utmost safety measure, we still put ourselves in harm's way and risked ourselves out there on the track. We did it for an uncommon and unusual love, derby love. Unless you have been a part of it, it's hard to understand. We knew the risks, and played anyway. We sacrificed time from our families, tightened our already crunched schedules and added derby into our jam packed lives.

There was a high cost, and we paid. We paid dearly and gladly. We contributed our talents, gifts and areas of expertise off the court, committing to 'jobs' that kept the league running and functioning like a viable business. As co-owners of the league, we all had a valuable stake in derby, particularly our own league. We took pride in that success and held on to a great sense of accomplishment.

We did all that while on the track learning new strategies. Calculating timing and angles for just the right hit, block or escape. Just like in life, these strategies mirror what we do daily off the track. Strategizing, working on our timing and angles in order to be successful. We use our critical thinking skills, math skills and our intelligence. We do this on and off the track. We don't play wild and haphazardly, and we don't live that way.

We did all that while tending to our bodies, nursing

SHEBA'S JAM

muscles, aches and pains, learning the difference between being injured and just being in pain. When we are injured, we have to remove ourselves and take time off to heal properly. Pain is just pain and usually a sign of growth and we can play through it. But knowing the difference is critical both on and off the track.

I won't even get into balancing roller derby, relationship, careers, family, home, personal issues, personal struggles, issues that are unique to the female body and everything else life brings. Just know that for many women, Roller Derby was a life line that gave us a special purpose and escape. It was a raft that kept some of us from sinking during a period in our lives when we really needed it. Now some of us, who no longer play, for whatever reason, have so much to draw on and reflect on a time when we were strong, courageous and basically warrior-like.

I hope this small tiny glimpse into roller derby from my world view adds some level of richness to your life, even if just a tab bit. It blessed my life tremendously!!

I wish each of you love, joy, fun times and great memory making in life!! Live to the fullest!!

Live John 10:10b!!

Sheba's Jam

Life Lessons

SHEBA'S JAM
Game Recognizes Game

People with certain likenesses often recognize each other. People with certain talents and gifts are quick to see the talent and gift in others. For example, people who skate well recognize other good skaters. People who are musically inclined recognize others with the same gift. Good cooks know good cooking. Skilled dancers have an eye for recognizing other good dancers. A good athlete knows another good athlete. Good preachers know good preaching. All the same, drug users seem to be able to spot out each other. Wickedness can see wickedness. Goodness knows goodness. And the list goes on.

A study I read once said that pretty people recognize other pretty people as though they are sizing up their competition. Some size up others and see them as a possible threat, while others assess whether others would make good comrades to be a part of a winning team. People are constantly assessing each other. Some people stand out and some are overlooked.

Let's define 'game' as participation in an activity that involves a special skill. Game recognizes the gift in someone even when they are not trying to show it off. Game comes naturally, even though practice and discipline enhance it. Game recognizes when someone is trying to have game but they really don't. Some people want game, but just don't have that gift or ability. They can try really hard and do all kinds of things to get it, but it's not really there and they cannot fool anyone into thinking they really have it. Some people can develop game if the foundation of gift is there. The bottom line is, when game is there, other game recognizes it. Sometimes, even your haters recognize it and they hate it.

The Bible talks about having the ability to recognize things spiritually. We should be able to recognize certain gifts and even spirits. I John 4 we are told to test the spirits to see whether they are from God (v.1) We should be able to recognize the Spirit of God (v.2). When God's Spirit is in you, you should be able to recognize when His Spirit is in someone else. You should also be able to recognize when His Spirit is NOT in someone. Verse 6 says, "We are from God, and whoever knows God listens to us; but whoever is not from God does not listen to us. This is how we recognize the Spirit of truth and the spirit of falsehood (NIV).

Game recognizes game. Spirit recognizes like spirit as well as opposing spirit. Sharpen your discernment skills so that you can recognize what and who you're dealing with. What are people seeing when they look at or listen to you? God bless.

Sheba's Jam
Don't Faint

Back in high school, I played basketball on the junior varsity team. I wasn't very good, but they let me be on the JV team. I got to travel with the team, build relationships with my teammates and have fun. I tried to keep up and it was a challenge, but I didn't give up. Running was hard for me and I wanted to be like those who it seemed to come easy to.

One summer I attended a girls basketball camp. I pushed my body hoping to increase my endurance. One day after camp, I went shopping with my mother. I can't remember if I had eaten or not. I remember feeling tired and funny while standing in line leaning on the cart. The next thing I remember is lying on the floor looking up at people frantically trying to help me and see if I was okay.

I had fainted. This wasn't the only time. There were some subsequent faints and I learned to be careful. My oldest daughter must have inherited this problem because as a child, she too had a few fainting spells. I was never diagnosed, but she was diagnosed with hypo-glycemia. She had to learn to keep her blood sugar up.

After the faint, we pretty much returned to normal, but it was a frightening experience for onlookers. Have you ever fainted? Just lost consciousness for a bit and passed out with no recollection of how you fell to the ground?

SHEBA'S JAM

In a nutshell, fainting is a temporary loss of consciousness or awareness. It's not death. Your heart still beats and blood still flows, but all thought processes momentarily cease. For that moment, you are motionless. You are not in control. You cannot make any moves and you appear to be dead even though you are not and suddenly you wake back up.

Physiologically, I cannot explain what causes fainting. A medical professional could tell you better than I could. I imagine that somewhere, something lacks, something misfires and you faint. The frightening thing is, sometimes it can sneak up on you. Other times however, you get signs that something is not right and you can avoid fainting. Sometimes it takes fainting to figure out the preceding feelings that indicate that a faint is coming on.

We understand physical fainting. What about spiritual fainting spells? Some of us faint in our spirit. We lose awareness of who and Whose we are during difficult times. We forget the power and authority we have access to. We forget our privileges as a child of God. We forget peace. We forget strength and courage. Sometimes we can spiritually black out for a minute. Thank God who can revive us.

Remember the children of Israel, when they wandered in the wilderness? They were hungry and thirsty, their soul fainted in them (Psa 107.5). They were in trouble, serious trouble. They thought they could die. Have you ever been there? What did they do then? They cried to the Lord and He delivered them (v. 6).

If you faint, pray. Jonah did. "When my soul fainted within me I remembered the Lord: and my prayer came unto thee, into thine holy temple" (Jonah 2.7). To prevent fainting, think on the goodness of the Lord like David did, "I had fainted, unless I had believed to see the goodness of the Lord in the land of the living (Psalm 27.13 KJV). Keep believing, knowing.

Don't forget God. Don't pass out in your spirit. Hold on to your God-consciousness no matter what the trouble is. Stay faithful to the task. "And let us not be weary in well doing: for in due season we shall reap, if we faint not." [Galatians 6.9 KJV]. Don't faint!

SHEBA'S JAM
Switching Gears

Have you ever unexpectedly had to switch gears? You had your mind on doing one thing and then you suddenly found yourself being called to do another. A sudden paradigm shift takes place and you end up doing the unexpected.

The Bible tells us in preaching, to always be ready, in season and out (2 Timothy 4:2). We never know what a situation will require of us due to an unexpected turn of events. Imagine young David, prior to becoming king in I Samuel 17.

David was sent to the battlefield simply for lunch delivery duty. He was a shepherd, not a warrior. He was dressed in plain clothes, not fighting gear. He was not planning to fight. He was not expecting to fight. His goal was to deliver food to the troops.

What if David was so focused on staying in his lane that he ignored the taunts of Goliath? What if David had decided to mind his own business and ignore the struggle? I can hear many of us thinking this if we were in David's place: "I'm not here to fight. They're on their own. They're trained for this, I'm not. I'm just here to bring food and that's all I'm doing. Plus, I'm not even dressed for it anyway, right? I'm not getting involved in their fight."

Sheba's Jam

We know that this situation was God's business and David couldn't help but notice and feel compelled to get involved even though that was not his initial purpose for being there that he knew of. Many times we see injustice and we turn a blind eye to it. But this was God's business, which makes it our business. We have to be aware and willing to step out of our lane sometimes and shift gears. Even when it's not 'our job,' there will be times we have to step up and step in for the people of God's sake. We have to be open to flowing with the shift and unexpected call of duty.

You never know how God is going to use you. You have to be open to flowing with His spirit. He just might change your plans, even if you're not dressed for it. Dressed for it or not, if God sends you, He will equip you and empower you to be victorious. Stay connected to Him always, so you will know when you need to step in and fight or simply walk away. Ask God for wisdom and use discernment. God just might have you switch gears.

SHEBA'S JAM
Spirit of Cooperation

I am blessed to have built some wonderful relationships. I am connected to some amazing people. As I pondered what has made these relationships such a blessing, this is what I came up with: "One of the keys to building great relationships is to be able to be supportive and helpful to people you believe in without worrying about what you can get out of the deal." When we learn to trust God with our faithfulness, He provides the reward that the people you helped could never provide, divine favor.

In order to be successful, you have to have good relationships with people because no one can succeed alone. We need each other's gifts and favor. We are a part of the same body with different gifts and blessings. We all compliment each other and we must work with a spirit of cooperation. When we do, we can accomplish great things! The Bible says, "Two are better off than one, because together they can work more effectively" (Ecc. 4:9 GNBDC).

This conference was successful because of relationships. Old relationships were strengthened and solidified and new relationships were formed and developed. We look forward to more great things happening in the future. I am praying for the relationships in your life. I pray that God gives you the wisdom to build great relationships that will contribute to your success and His plan for your life. We all need each other. We should focus less on competition and more on unity. "Behold, how good and

Sheba's Jam

pleasant it is when brethren (and sisters) dwell in unity" (Psalm 133:1). Praying for an increase in the spirit of cooperation.

SHEBA'S JAM
POSTURE

"You were sitting there with your back straight and your smile was amazing!" He said.

"That's why you spoke to me?" she replied.

"It drew me," he added.

Her body language said she was confident. Her smile indicated happiness. He saw a secure woman with feminine charm; joyful and fulfilled. He wanted to know more.

Nonverbal communication speaks volumes. Good posture tells that you care and you're holding it together. Posture can determine how others respond to your presence before they hear you speak. Men notice the posture of a woman.

God notices and responds to our posture too. The way we come before His presence matters. Prayer posture, on our knees, with a bowed down head and clasped hands, speaks humility, reverence, submission and honor. In praise and worship, our lifted hands express our desire to reach Him, positioned to receive. Our tears express how God touches our hearts.

The King of Kings is worthy of our effort to come before His presence whether we kneel, stand, sit, lie down or prostrate. What's more important than our physical posture is the posture of our heart, humble and broken before Him. God notices.

Posture is how you present your body as well as your heart. It's important. At all times: "...present your bodies a living sacrifice, holy, acceptable unto God, which is your reasonable service." (Rom. 12.1)

Always mind your posture; back straight, head up, God's love in your heart. Let good posture become a natural part of who you are.

Sheba's Jam
Grand Slam

I am not an avid baseball fan. However, being a former softball player, I am familiar with the basics. Driving in the car one day, with my friend riding shotgun and my children in the back seat, we listened to a Detroit Tiger game on the radio.

The announcer announced that the bases were loaded and a batter was up. It became a tense moment full of possibility. It's one thing to hit a home run, it's another thing to hit a home run while the bases are loaded!

He did it! He hit a home run! "It's a GRAND SLAM!!" I yelled along with the announcer.

"What's a grand slam mom?" my son asked.

"It's when all the bases have a man on them, which is called 'bases loaded, and when the batter hits a home run, all four men come home and each score a point," I tried to explain. One hit scores four points!" I explained.

In our lives, some of us have our bases loaded. We have been lining things up, putting things in their proper place. We have taken some classes. We have read books and the Bible trying to prepare ourselves. We've been studying and applying ourselves trying to do better in life. We have networked, fasted, prayed, treated our neighbor better, sowed into good ground, and done all that we know to do to reap a harvest and be blessed.

Some of us are tapping our feet looking up toward heaven wondering, 'When God when?' Possibilities have been piling up. Expectations are accumulating. You are so close to a breakthrough, you can taste it! You feel like you're ready to burst, because you see the potential for a windfall of blessings right there in front of you.

So now you're up to bat. This could really be 'it'! Your bases are loaded. If only you can knock this opportunity out of the ballpark, it will be your grand slam! I pray that God will guide your hands as you take that big swing!!! I pray that God will bless the work of your hands and that you will reap your due reward!

Be faithful! A faithful person shall abound with blessings! (Prov. 28.20). Your hard work and dedication will pay off. God is not mocked, whatever you sow, you will reap (Gal. 6.7). Don't get tired of doing good, in due season, you will reap if you don't faint (Gal. 6.9). Keep at it, because your grand slam is near

Sheba's Jam
Power in Partnership

There was a cartoon in the 1970s called Super Friends. Super Friends consisted of a variety of super heroes. Among the heroes was a set of twins, a male and a female. When trouble came, the twins would do a clenched fist high five and chant, "Wonder Twin Powers Activate!" Then they would go on to request what form they would like to take on in order to accomplish the task at hand.

There was power and purpose in their partnership. They recognized it, experienced it and used it to conquer. In battle, with our Rock, our Lord, one can chase off a thousand and 'two' can put ten thousand to flight (Deut. 32:30). Do the math. There is power in partnership. God says that where two (or three) believers are gathered together in His name, He is there (Matt. 18:20). Together, we invoke His presence, which gives us His power.

There are powerful partnerships in the Bible where comrades help each other. Think about Naomi and Ruth. After losing her husband and two sons, Naomi was ready to give up, thinking there was no hope for her (Ruth 1). She sent her daughters in law off since there was still hope for them to have a better life. She was going to remain behind and perhaps simply exist or lay down and die. But Ruth refused to leave. Ruth refused to give up on her. Ruth insisted on staying by her side and in doing that, she gave Naomi purpose in life again. Naomi poured into Ruth and mentored her. This training enabled Ruth to land Boaz. Ruth helped Naomi realize purpose in her being.

We all need a Ruth in our lives when there seems to be no hope for us in our situations. Just the same, sometimes we have to be like Ruth, to those who feel hopeless. Like Bill Withers sang in his song from the 1970s, "We all need somebody to lean on." Moses needed Aaron and Hur when his arms got tired and they held them up for him. As a result Joshua led the victory over the Amalekites (Exodus 17).

There is power in partnership. The Lord God said, it is not good for man to be alone (Genesis 2:18). We all need our personal time. But then we cannot neglect coming together to exhort each other (Hebrews 10:25). Partner with those who love your heart and care about your well-being. Good partners are transparent and honest. Steer clear of opportunists, leeches, deceivers and liars. They will try to destroy you. True partners build each other up. Keep God in the center of it all. Pray together and be on one accord. Blend and mesh operating as a single unit with one mind, the mind of Christ. Grab your twin, do the clenched fist high five like Michelle and Barack did and: ACTIVATE! "In the form of: MORE THAN CONQUERORS IN CHRIST JESUS!" May your godly partnerships be blessed.

Seek. Then get your oil and work it like you're spraying activator trying to get your 'curl' nice and juicy! May your blessings drip with overflow!!! Get on your knees

SHEBA'S JAM

and pray, then ACTIVATE so the power can be released!!! May blessings be activated in your life by the good things you do.

Sheba's Jam
70 x 7

There's a skater whose number is 70x7. When I saw her jersey, I had to acknowledge it.

"Does that mean what I think it means?" I asked.

"Yup! Those who know the Word know," she replied.

Forgiveness.

Even though most of us know that we are required to forgive in order to be forgiven (Luke 6:37), forgiveness is among our biggest struggles.

Sometimes it's hard to differentiate between forgiving and enabling. Sometimes we think that if we forgive, we are saying that the action was okay. It can feel like you're giving the offender a 'pass.' When we suffer, we want the person who caused it to pay!

It's easy to forget the innumerable times that God has 'covered' us with not only forgiveness, but spared us of ill consequences of our offenses. We love the idea of forgiveness when it is us being forgiven.

However, when forgiveness requires something of us, it is more of a challenge. It is especially hard when you have not healed from the hurt. It's harder to forgive while you are suffering from what an offender has done to you. Read Matthew 18:32-33.

When we do forgive, we can see maybe once, twice or a few times. One day Peter was fed up and tired of forgiving and asked if there was a limit on the number of times one should be forgiven. So he decided to ask Jesus. He thought seven was a fair number. (Matt. 18:21)

I would imagine he was disappointed with Jesus' response: "I tell you NOT up to seven times, but seventy times seven" (Matt. 18:22).

If I were that guy, I might have thought, "Seriously? That's too many!"

But it's not our call to make. Jesus said it and it implies that forgiveness is without limit. If there were a limit, I am confident that most of us would be maxed out with Him!

That is not to say that we should be doormats allowing ourselves to be abused. We don't have to associate or deal with people who repeatedly offend or harm us. That can be costly. But we cannot carry bitterness in our heart. Forgive and let go.

Sometimes it's a process. It can be hard to forgive while you're in deep pain. At least move in the right direction toward forgiveness with a mind to forgive.

Forgive. 70x7.

SHEBA'S JAM
Over and Back

I'm not a huge sports fan, but put my son, daughter, niece or nephew in a game, and I'm all in with bells on. I'm their number one fan! I will watch them attentively and cheer them on as loudly as possible. A couple of weeks ago, I had the pleasure of watching my beautiful niece play basketball at one of her games. They remained undefeated, 6 and 0. As I watched the game, I reminisced on my days as a JV basketball player at RRHS in the 1980s. The rules of the game resurfaced in my mind. Unlike my sister, the basketball coach mom, I needed a refresher.

One call that stood out to me that day as I watched was 'over and back.' If a player crosses over the midcourt line and goes back over it in the other direction, the whistle blows and the team is penalized for it. Once the midcourt line is crossed, you cannot back up and then go back forward. You just cannot get away with that in the game of basketball.

It made me think about life. There are some lines in life that you cannot cross and go back. Sometimes there is a point of no return. When you cross the line, there is a penalty. When you do certain things in life, sometimes you cannot go back to the way you were before crossing over. That one sexual encounter that gave you a lifelong condition cannot be reversed. The one time use of a needle changed your blood forever. The one act of murder will be forever etched in your mind. The betrayal of someone's trust forever changes their perception of you. Once you cross over, you cannot go back. Some things do go on your permanent record and hinder you.

We can be forgiven by people. We can try to work it out. However, what happened can never be erased and neither can the effects of it. The blow may be softened, but sometimes consequences are inevitable, no matter how sorry we are or how much we repent or apologize. The damage is done and it's irreversible. We have to live with that.

Don't fret. All is not lost. Even when we go over and try to go back, we pay our penalty, we can still live. After all, life does go on. God is so good. In spite of the fact we are penalized for crossing forbidden lines, God provides for us. "All things work together....." (Romans 8:28), even our mess can work for us if we play our cards right. Live and learn. Help others avoid the bad choices you have made.

We can breathe a lot easier knowing that even though we are penalized and chastened on this earth, our Father in heaven forgives us completely and blots out our offenses entirely, as far as the east is from the west (Psalm 103:12). He remembers them no more. He holds nothing against us and we are cleansed of all unrighteousness (I John 1:9). His shed blood does all that for us. Therefore, we can REJOICE! He forgives and He forgets. So live. Live your best life, condemnation-free! Abundantly!

Sheba's Jam
.Calluses

A lot of us use our hands and feet for work and or play. When my son was doing gymnastics, his hands became really sore from the pressure of swinging on the bars. He was in a lot of pain and when he told his instructor, the instructor said, 'good.'

He said it was good because that meant my son's skin was thickening and developing a protective layer of harder skin. This makes pressure more tolerable. I have the same issue on my feet. As a skater, the pressure points under my feet have calluses.

Maybe you have noticed calluses on your hands or feet from friction and pressure. People who work hard with their hands usually have what people call 'rough' hands. People who wear bad shoes or are hard on their feet have 'rough' feet. Sometimes you can look at a person's hands or feet and see that they've been through a lot. Calluses don't just show up for no reason.

Sometimes I notice that people who go through a lot in life, people who have been hurt repeatedly and experience a lot of friction and pressure come off as 'hardened'. The harsh repetitious pain in their lives causes them to get that way. It's a defense or coping mechanism.

When I see this in people, while I do understand how they become this way, I say it is 'not 'necessarily good.

Sheba's Jam

People do what they have to do to survive, physically and emotionally. We are hardwired to fight to live.

While it is good to develop 'tough skin' emotionally, it is not good to develop a 'hardened heart.' We have to know the difference between the two. Tough skin is when we learn not to allow certain things to bother or hurt us. It's when we're able to keep focus no matter what is thrown at us and the hits don't hurt so badly. Tough skin is good when you still have a soft heart.

A soft heart still cares even though the exterior tough skin is tough enough to protect it. When a heart becomes hardened, it means you really don't care anymore. A hardened heart has the potential to become ruthless, void of compassion and cruel. If you ever feel yourself going there, then pray. When you see others there, pray.

If we ask and if we're willing, we know that God can '...give you a new heart and put a new spirit in you; He will remove from you your heart of stone and give you a heart of flesh." (Eze. 36:26) God is able to touch and heal a hardened heart.

Sheba's Jam
The Firm

Johann Wolfgang von Goethe once said, "She who is firm in will, molds the world to herself [modified]. It reminds me of Romans 12:2 which says, "Be not conformed to this world…"

A strong [firm] willed person does not give in. They stand firm in their conviction. When your life demonstrates firmness, people will stop coming to you with nonsense trying to sway you. People will try you. Depending on your reaction, they will either get you to conform, keep trying if they think there's a possibility you will conform, or they will quit and leave you alone. Resist the devil and he will flee from you [James 4:7]. It takes a firm will to resist temptation.

Peer pressure and similar tactics work to get people to do things they should not do. Some people go as far as using coercion or force to make people conform. In those cases the will is violated and that's beyond your control. But when we have a choice, it takes a disciplined and well trained person to maintain a firm will.

Typically, people treat you based on how you carry yourself. Predators can smell fear, timidity and desperation. When your will is firm no matter what, predators may see it as a challenge, but will eventually give up. But just like when the devil flees, he goes away for a time to plot a different way to come back at you and knock you off your square. Stay on point. Don't waver. When you waver, you are like a wave of the sea driven and tossed [James 1:6]. Be firm.

SHEBA'S JAM

People shouldn't be influencing you, you should be influencing them. You should be the trend setter. When this happens, you are molding the world, it's not molding you. You should not want to be like other people, they will want to be godly like you. It takes courage to be different. You are peculiar [Titus 2:14, I Peter 2:9]. Your conduct is interesting and magnetic. People want what you have. That's how you really win people over, by living the life you talk about. Ask yourself, "Is my will firm or am I easily persuaded?" "Am I molding the world or is it molding me?" Be like David and say, "I shall not be moved" [Psalm 16:8, 62:6, Acts 2:25] Be a part of a wonderful group of people; the faithful, THE FIRM.

Sheba's Jam
Teamwork

I very often say, "Two heads are better than one." I am humble and wise enough to know that I can't think of everything. I am always grateful when someone else shares a great idea with me. I don't know everything. I'm not good at everything. I can't see everything. It's good to be partnered with others who can do the things that I cannot.

That's why a great team is powerful. Each gifted in his or her own area of specialty and together they sync up to accomplish a common goal. I love the X-Men series because it illustrates that concept. Cerebro and Magneto knew how to put a great team together. They chose people with the best gifts and talents. Members varied, but came together, operating in their own gift, to do one thing: succeed as a unit. It makes me think of how the body works and the Body of Christ (I Cor. 12).

There is power in unity and in numbers. No one member is any more important than another. Faithfulness is essential. Teammates are gifted uniquely and complement each other. That makes a team strong. Some might call this kind of team, a 'dream team.' Whether it is a sports team, a workforce, family, church, crew, etc... Dream teams win by making things happen. When Apollos and Paul worked together, one planted, the other watered and God gave the increase (1 Cor. 3:6). The key component to making their team produce what that God was a part of it. You need God on your team if it will do anything fruitful.

Sheba's Jam

The main person I want on my team is God. If God is not on the team, I'd have to quit. God is the source Who makes good things happen. As I work with God, I want to be the best I can be. I don't want to be a weak link. However, on a really good team, even if you're a weak link for a season, the rest of the team is able and willing to cover you as you get yourself together.

I want to be an effective part of the team; a contributing factor. I want to be one that my teammates are proud and grateful to work with. I can do this by working unusually exceptionally hard, perfecting my craft.

When people do unusually exceptional work with their gift, they eventually become a hot commodity. We're all capable. It just takes commitment. Are you exercising your gift(s)? Are you the kind of person someone would want on their team? God wants to recruit you because

God put something special on the inside of you that the Kingdom can benefit from. I just hope you recognize it, are faithful to it and work unusually hard at it. Welcome to the team. Your teamwork is needed and really appreciated.

Sheba's Jam
Coach

When you hear the word 'coach,' I hope the first thing you think of is not a purse. What is a coach? A coach is a trainer, a teacher or instructor. They teach, train, prepare and instruct. They motivate, inspire, encourage and get people into motion. They can bring out the best in people. They can bring out greatness that people never knew they had inside of them.

A coach will celebrate you when you are on the right path and victorious. A coach will encourage you to rise when you fall. They will help you to see your faults when you're wrong, not to rub your nose in it, but to show you the right way. A coach can see greatness in you that you are not able to see yourself. Coaches are visionaries who believe in the potential and possibilities of those on their team.

Some coaches are dedicated, while others are half hearted. But let's hear it for the dedicated coaches who know how to bring out the best in people. Thanks to all the coaches who commit their time and energy into helping others succeed and celebrating them as they win. Thanks for imparting wisdom and guidance.

Thanks for being on the team. Maybe you're not an athlete or other team member, but who coaches you in life? Life is like a game and too many are losing because they have not been coached properly. Maybe others gave up on them or they gave up on themselves and no one was there to encourage them and remind them of their potential. Maybe you don't have a life coach. Here's how you can get one: Read the Word. It's a manual. The ultimate coach was Jesus. He is our Shepherd. He coached the Twelve Disciples. They didn't always get it right, but He continued to work with them, teaching them.

While He is not on earth physically, He has designated under-shepherds in the form of Prophets, Apostles, Pastors, Teachers, Evangelists, to coach you in this life (Eph. 4:11). They've been sent to perfect you (v. 12). Preachers have been sent to speak to us (Rom. 10:15).

Whether you coach or need to be coached, get in the game. The outcome has already been determined. With Christ, you win!

Sheba's Jam
Backpack

Imagine living your life carrying a backpack on your back. For some odd reason, you never unzipped the backpack to see what was inside. You just carried it around because it's what you've always done. It's all people around you have done. You just carried the backpack. A few people suggested that you unzip it, but you were afraid that it would require something of you. Rather than sacrifice things you were comfortable with, you let well enough alone.

Many days you struggled and lacked resources. You tried to muster up resources to get things you needed, but always came up short. There was always a nagging feeling that something was missing. It even crossed your mind that what was missing might be inside the backpack. But nahhh, you left the backpack zipped up.

At the end of your life, you find out that everything you needed was in the backpack. It contained resources that could have made your life more joyful, fulfilling, and abundant. You would have still had problems, but the backpack was filled with remedies. Man, if you could only do it all over again.

Now imagine that the backpack is Jesus. Maybe you already know Him. Through prayer, you unzip the backpack and He shows you the way to abundant life, life in all its fullness. Read John 10:10. He offers healing, salvation, guidance, courage, strength, peace, joy, comfort, wisdom, provision, and so much more. If you don't know Him, He is saying, "Here I am! I stand at the door and knock. If you hear my voice and open the door, I will come in..." (Rev. 3:20).

You have access. Don't live your life without using what Jesus offers. Don't be remorseful at the end of your life. Receive Him and all that He offers right now.

SHEBA'S JAM
Victor

Victor is more than my uncle's name. Victor is what a person is when they have victory! It's the opposite of victim. Victors are winners! Victors are successful! Victors are optimistic and just like everyone else; Victors face unfair challenges, problems, heartache, pain and struggle.

We all have troubles and things that come fiercely against us. So why are some of us victors and others victims? I think it's a state of mind. People with a victim mentality, often sulk and complain. Most of us already know that life is not fair. Even with that being so, and knowing that the odds are stacked up against us, we can still have a victorious state of mind.

We can do this when we remember who and whose we are. You can choose to believe that you were born to lose or born to win. I choose the latter. I may come up short sometimes, but I refuse to surrender. Life isn't fair, and neither is favor. You have to believe that you walk in the favor of God. You have to believe that God wants you to be a winner. Remember that Jesus said, "I came that you might have life abundantly." That sounds like a winner. On the other hand, we know that the thief (devil) came to steal, kill and destroy (John 10:10). Choose Jesus' plan. Even when the thief steals from you, God is able to provide and restore.

I want to be on the winning side and I want you to be victorious with me. We don't have time to groan and

105

complain. Victims often die while they whine and moan. Don't lie there, get up before you get stomped on!

Even when things don't go our way, even when we make mistakes, or even when we are severely victimized, we have to believe that "all things work together for good for those who love Him and are called to His purpose" -that would be you (Romans 8:28). As a victor you can stand on the fact that 'no weapon that is formed against you shall prosper (Isaiah 54:17). You are unstoppable. Be prayerful and sensitive to how God communicates His will and actions to you.

You were born to win. Are you in it to win it? You have a choice. You can choose to be a victor or a victim. You may be down, but you don't have to be out. Get up. There is a victor in you. God wired you that way, so get up and live like it.

Sheba's Jam
Small Army

I am fascinated by movies that involve battle. There is something about the art of war, how people fight. What do victors have in common?

I like watching the virtue of goodness prevail over evil. I have watched many war movies about Vietnam and other war and battle movies. Gladiator is a favorite. Black Hawk Down, Full Metal Jacket, Hamburger Hill and other war movies have enlightened my perspective on the spirit of the human warrior. Although sci-fi, I enjoyed Lara Croft Tomb Raider because this woman conquered things that appeared insurmountable.

I was recently watching the warriors of Sparta in the movie 300. I watched them relentlessly defeat armies of thousands. They were out-numbered, but not overpowered. It reminded me of Gideon (Judges 7). Gideon also went to battle with just 300 men. They too went up against thousands. Gideon started out with 20k. God said that was too many. After a process of elimination, Gideon was down to 10k. Still too many, God said. So after a test of how they would drink water, the army was down to 300.

Finally, something God could work with. God needed the army to be small because He didn't want them to think it was their strength (due to large numbers) that caused them to win. God wanted them to know that He was the reason for their victory (v.2).

It's amazing what God can do with small numbers. God gives victory. He delights in doing great things with small things. The Bible says, "But God hath chosen the foolish things of the world to confound the wise; and God hath chosen the weak things of the world to confound the things which are mighty." (I Corinthians 1:27KJV)

I believe this applies across the board. God can do big things with a small church. He can do a lot with a little bit of money. He can maximize the use of small space. You can do great things at your small job. You can learn a lot at your small school. You can change a big world with your small voice. He can create a big dream from your small idea. God loves to show off. He likes to reinforce the fact that He is God and there is none above Him. When He operates in the small things, you know it's Him causing the victory, and not man's might.

In a culture that associates big numbers with success and God's blessing, it's hard for some to understand how or why God could choose to use something small to conquer great things. Maybe you're small, and your mountain is big. Tell it to move and jump in the sea, and it will (Matthew 21:21). Your army may be small, or your army may just consist of you, but with God on your side, your army is mighty! They better watch out now! Like the U of M freshmen fab five used to say: "Shock the world."

Sheba's Jam
Pace Yourself

In the aftermath of a recent snowstorm in Detroit , I was driving. I spend a lot of time on the road and I have learned to be very cautious where road conditions are concerned. On this particular day, I did not feel a lot of traction, so I reduced my speed.

Driving down a relatively major street, I noticed a vehicle in my rear view mirror that was right on my tail. It's as though the driver were trying to push me along, attempting to force me to speed up.

Knowing my own personal comfort level with my vehicle, I maintained my speed despite the disdain of the driver behind me. I refuse to wreck my vehicle because of another person's impatience. I'd rather arrive late than to not arrive at all. My only hope for the driver behind me was that their need to drive quickly was not dire.

There was only one drivable lane. Desperate to get around me, the driver behind me drove over snow to pass me. Honestly, I was happy for the driver if that's what they really wanted to do. I had no remorse for standing my ground and minding my safety. It was not long before the vehicle was out of my sight, far ahead.

I continued to drive along and I saw a vehicle that had run off the road and was lodged in a snowbank. The passengers were outside the vehicle trying to figure out how they would get their vehicle out. They looked baffled and frustrated. Probably in need of a tow which could take hours. Guess who it was? It was the vehicle that sped around me. It looks like they were in a hurry to get nowhere fast. If only they could have relaxed and exercised the fruit of patience.

Sometimes in life, when conditions require it, we have to slow it down. In some seasons we have to simply coast along. Applying the gas for speed could be detrimental. Some people might come along and pressure you to go faster, touting, "You should be much further along than you are!" They try to make you feel bad about your lack of progress without taking into consideration the conditions that surround your life. Being slothful is one thing, pacing yourself is truly another.

We all need an encouraging nudge sometimes. It's great when friends care about us and want us to be at our best. They may take it upon themselves to push us along. That's a nice gesture and sometimes it's a good thing, but sometimes circumstances in our lives require us to take it slow. A wise man once told me that you must, "Know thyself." Only you know what you can do safely and what pace works for you. Don't let people pressure you or make you feel like you are not progressing enough. Don't compare your progress to the progress of others or like you have to keep up. You just might pass them by while they're stuck somewhere.

Going at a pace that is more than your situation can handle could cause you to lose control. Trying to keep up with the Jones' can land you in a ditch, stuck. Participating in a rat race being fiercely competitive can cause you to crash and burn. Be cautious, not reckless. Think things through. Be cognizant. Move accordingly.

Sometimes God will put you on a fast track. If He does, surely He will equip you for it. Surely, God will make your environment conducive to such speed, for your own safety. I'm not suggesting or encouraging complacency or laziness, but caution. Remember what the Bible says: "...the race is not given to the swift or the battle to the strong... (Ecc. 9:11). But the one who stands firm to the end will be saved (Matt. 24:13). Pace yourself.

SHEBA'S JAM
Leadership

Oftentimes, in order to bring a vision to pass, visionaries have to take the lead in carrying out the plans for their vision. Most visionaries end up being leaders.

Usually when you think of a leader, you think of someone who is in charge of something (usually a group) and has followers (members). A leader is generally defined as one who goes forward, or one who guides.

I believe that even if you are not the head, president or leader of a group or organization, you can still have leadership skills and qualities. I believe that a leader is someone who is first of all able to lead him/herself as an individual and can lead by example.

You can be a leader in your home, in your family, in school, or on the job. Leading usually means that you bring great ideas and contributions to the table for your group or vision while being open to the ideas and contributions of others. It means that you can handle responsibility, you have earned the respect of others, and you give respect to others.

A leader stands up for what is right even if they have to stand alone. Leaders take initiative. They are able to persuade others to see their point of view because they are good communicators and can make others catch their vision. The best leaders are humbly led by the Holy

Sheba's Jam

Spirit. "For as many as are led by the Spirit of God, these are sons of God" (Romans 8:14 NKJV).

A leader should be wise with Godly wisdom. A good leader knows what his/her goals are and makes a plan accordingly. Jesus asked, 'Can the blind lead the blind? Will they not both fall in the ditch?" (Luke 6:39 NKJV)

Strive to be a good leader whether you lead ten or ten thousand. Pray for guidance from the Holy Spirit. Please remember your leaders in your prayers. Our leaders need our sincere prayers for their strength and wisdom to make the right decisions on our behalf.

As glamorous as it may appear to be a leader, being a leader carries huge responsibility. So, please pray for your leaders. Pray for Pastors everywhere while you also pray for yourself to be a good leader or steward over what God has given you.

SHEBA'S JAM
Build Confidence

Many destinies have gone unfulfilled due to the lack of confidence. Some of us have passed up opportunities because we did not feel qualified or worthy. Truthfully, none of us are qualified or worthy, but by the grace of God. Many of us have been so intimidated by a big dream or huge task, that we concluded that it would be much easier to just stick with the status quo and let the cards fall as they may. Many of us are afraid to risk failure or hardship.

Fulfilling destiny is no easy task. In order to fulfill destiny, you must be strong and courageous. This phrase is repeated in the Bible several times, particularly when God was dealing with Joshua. Joshua had a big task in front of him and God knew he would need strength and courage to tackle it.

Maybe there is a big task before you that will ultimately glorify God and it seems intimidating and overwhelming. Be strong and courageous. Build your confidence by building your relationship with God. Get to know what His Word says and pray daily. Make God a part of your life and remember Him in every thought that enters your mind. Pray for wisdom and guidance.

When God is an integral part of your life and there is communication going on through earnest prayer, you can have the confidence you need to succeed in whatever God puts before you. God will give you the power to do the impossible and you will utterly shock the world with the brilliance God has placed inside of you. Hold your head up high and know that God is and He is with you in all that you do (when you're doing what's right).

Then you will walk in your way securely and in confident trust, and you shall not dash you foot or stumble (Proverbs 3:23). For the Lord shall be your confidence, firm and strong, and shall keep your foot from being caught in a trap or some hidden danger (Proverbs 3:26).

Sheba's Jam
Journal Therapy

A couple years ago, when I was taking a class for women in ministry, one of the requirements was that we keep a daily prayer journal for thirty days. When I first heard we had to do this, I didn't know how I was going to find time to make journal entries every day. Begrudgingly, I started writing in my journal.

I wrote about situations that were going on and how I wanted the Lord to help me. Some of the things were not pleasant to see on paper. I wrote about it anyway. The more I wrote in my journal, the easier it became. It was like I began exposing my innermost thoughts and feelings and I was forced to look at the real me. To my surprise, getting these feelings out of my system and on to paper was great therapy. It was a way of releasing baggage in my life. I was letting it out. Sometimes, when it's too hard to talk or you have no one to confide in, the next best thing is to write it out.

As the days went by, I could see changes in my feelings and thoughts. Sometimes I felt better and sometimes I felt more confused. But still, I felt like I was getting closer to God because I was letting Him know what was going on and I was releasing a lot of pain and confusion. I wrote a few poems as a result.

I was glad I got this assignment, because on my own, I may have never considered writing a journal. It forced me to take a deeper look inside and it brought out some things. I even used some of the writing to put in my book, "*Voice of Transition*".

You don't have to make journal entries every single day, but try writing something at least once a week, reflecting on your life, prayers, and walk with the Lord. You never know, your testimony could result in you writing your own book. Is there a book inside of you? Even if you don't write or publish a book, writing is one of the best therapies I know of.

Sheba's Jam
Journal

Take moments to reflect on how your hobbies, your work and other things you do affect your outlook on life. What makes you learn and grow? Why and how?

Use these ruled pages to be introspective and ponder the parallels between life, your activities, your faith and your spirituality. Grow in wisdom and enhance your life.

Sheba's Jam

Sheba's Jam

SHEBA'S JAM

Sheba's Jam

SHEBA'S JAM

Sheba's Jam

Sheba's Jam

Sheba's Jam

SHEBA'S JAM

SHEBA'S JAM

Sheba's Jam

SHEBA'S JAM

SHEBA'S JAM

Sheba's Jam

Sheba's Jam

Sheba's Jam

SHEBA'S JAM

Sheba's Jam

Sheba's Jam

SHEBA'S JAM

Sheba's Jam

Sheba's Jam

SHEBA'S JAM

Sheba's Jam

Sheba's Jam

SHEBA'S JAM

Sheba's Jam

Sheba's Jam

Sheba's Jam

Sheba's Jam

Sheba's Jam

Sheba's Jam

_____
_____
_____
_____
_____
_____
_____
_____
_____
_____
_____
_____
_____
_____
_____
_____
_____
_____
_____
_____
_____
_____
_____
_____
_____
_____